HAPPINESS

HAPPINESS

POEMS BY DEBORAH KEENAN

COFFEE HOUSE PRESS :: MINNEAPOLIS

Book design and cover art by Leslie Ross

Back cover photograph by Tim Francisco

The author gratefully acknowledges the following journals and magazines where many of these poems, some in slightly different versions, first appeared. "Open Hands," "The City," and "What It Was Like Today" first appeared in *Caliban*; "Lilacs and Hail," "What Drives Us," "Nothing to Eat," and "Architecture" first appeared in *Shenandoah*; "Stigmata" first appeared in *Painted Bride Quarterly*; "Loving Motels," "Burning," and "Wrong" first appeared in *Minnesota Monthly*; "Comfort" first appeared in *Kentucky Poetry Review*; "Mothers" and "The Autobiography of Clothes" first appeared in *Great River Review*; "The Snow Woman," "Small History," "Against the Good," "Fox," "Marriage," "To Live Without," "Rogue Wave," and "White Mittens" first appeared in the *Santa Monica Review*.

The publisher would like to thank the following funders for assistance that helped make this book possible: The Andrew W. Mellon Foundation; The McKnight Foundation; the National Endowment for the Arts, a federal agency; the Jerome Foundation; the Lannan Foundation; Dayton Hudson Foundation on behalf of Dayton's and Target Stores; the General Mills Foundation; The St. Paul Companies; the Star Tribune/Cowles Media Company; the Honeywell Foundation; and The Prudential Foundation. This activity is made possible in part by a grant provided by the Minnesota State Arts Board, through an appropriation by the Minnesota State Legislature.

Coffee House Press books are available to the trade through our primary distributor, Consortium Book Sales & Distribution, 1045 Westgate Drive, Saint Paul, MN 55114. Our books are also available through all major library distributors and jobbers, and through most small press distributors, including Bookpeople, Inland, and Small Press Distribution. For personal orders, catalogs or other information, write to:
Coffee House Press
27 North Fourth Street, Suite 400, Minneapolis, MN 55401

Library of Congress CIP data
Keenan, Deborah.
    Happiness : poems / by Deborah Keenan.
      p. cm.
    ISBN 1-56689-033-0
    I. Title.
PS3561.E36H37 1995   94-45620
811'.54—DC20   CIP

Special thanks to Jim Krusoe and Dabney Stuart, poets and editors.

The author also wishes to thank The Bush Foundation for a Fellowship in poetry, the National Endowment for the Arts for a Fellowship in poetry, and The Loft for financial and spiritual support. Special gratitude to Roseann Lloyd, Jim Moore, Margaret Hasse, Patricia Kirkpatrick, Don Brunnquell, Michael Moos, Lon Otto, Jean Adams, and Laurie Kemp. My gratitude to all my students who remind me daily of the power and grace of poetry and friendship.

Much love, many blessings, many thanks to Stephen Seidel, Brendan Keenan, Molly Keenan, Joe Seidel, Cordelia Seidel, Pat Francisco, and Mary Rockcastle.

For my brothers,
Daniel Clifford Bowman & Larry Wells Bowman
"and they were brothers from paradise . . ."
& for Jim Moore

Contents

SECTION V: WHAT IT WAS LIKE TODAY

SECTION I—SMALL HISTORY

Small History

She said it, she said,
"If I can't say something truthful
then I'm not going to talk."

I am going to make myself a small history. I am going to tell
and not show, show and not tell.

The smallness will be its beauty. There's a girl whose oldest
brother's dogs always died violently. Can you see her brother

walking up the dead-end street, another golden dog dead in his
arms, and the mother says, "He must have gotten into the

neighbor's poison." The boy is crying hard. He probably should
cry this hard every couple of months but the girl doesn't think

he's cried in years. The girl thinks the neighbors keep poison
and she still thinks that. This is history.

This small girl never had a dog that was her dog until it was
almost too late to love dogs the way her brother did.

When she finally got a dog she had to leave town, she flew all
the way to Athens, then in the middle of the night she got on

the smallest plane in the sky and went to an island to live.
She was sixteen and her dog was back home. She didn't think

about the dog at all, but in an old letter her mother saved
she sees her erratic teenage handwriting—"Give Garf a pat

for me." Named for Garfunkel. Now that dog is dead, but she
gave him away long before to a man whose job it was to

walk all the parks and protected forests in her hometown.
He was just supposed to walk and notice things. Her dog was

happy. On this island so many years ago a man told her she was
beautiful. Another man held her hand every night at the outdoor

movie theater where she watched *Suddenly Last Summer* dubbed
in Greek, and crazy Italian movies dubbed in Greek,

and really, she saw the worst movies she'd ever seen that
summer, under stars that were huge and fell constantly.

On the island so many years ago one man gave her a necklace
with a silver madonna swinging from the chain, and another

man gave her flowers every day at the same café where she sat
writing letters home, reading, while everyone else slept

the hot afternoons away. She calls this her summer of men.
How strange they were to love her, adore her, make up pet

names for her. To her mother, as a baby she'd been an object
of beauty, the desired girl, she has always understood that.

On the island, to be purely an object of desire in a summer
of ecstatic heat and sunlight—she felt holy and carnal.

She has saved her paintings from that time, timid brushstrokes,
the perfect reflection of her fear and desire waking at once.

The father of the family who petted her in her sleep, and when
she woke to his strokes he said, "Shshshshshsh."

The young revolutionaries who told her to swim far out into the
Aegean so they could tell her in broken English about the junta,

the older brother imprisoned, the cousin disappeared, would she
carry the word back home to her America?

"Yes," she said, but no one cared too much when she did, such a
small disturbance on the planet, and Vietnam claimed the light

when she got off the airplane and was American again. She has
this picture in her mind of her middle brother telling her to

read *The Stranger*. She is twelve and she reads all night. The
kind of heat in that book is what she finds when she arrives

in Corfu four years later. She did not believe in that kind of
heat until she felt it on her skin. Did she think Camus was

a liar? No, she had only thought the word "fiction." She is
desperately attracted to that kind of heat. Later, when she

spends a year living in Scotland, she cannot believe it never
gets warm. Somewhere she'd decided that crossing an ocean

meant access to heat. In the middle of the most beautiful
country she is inconsolable; there is nothing warm in Scotland

except her home. She shakes with the cold in other people's
houses. She weeps when she goes out walking, the fog and mist

are furry, she feels pressed with all this moisture, her body
fat with cold and damp. After she read Camus all those years

ago she knew she would never kill anyone. But in Scotland,
after she gives birth to her first son, she admits she will

kill anyone who tries to harm this new child. She accepts
this as a reasonable change of heart. In Corfu, all the heat

got tangled up with all the desire and all the beauty, and
because she was called beautiful she decided the heat made her

that way. In Scotland, she wears the same dress for months.
It is a pale, apple-green color. She has wanted to describe

this dress, its true color, for half her life now. It is not
enough to say "apple-green." It is not enough to add the word

pale. Now she spends time trying to paint the color of this
corduroy dress. She searches art stores for the right colored

pencil, the right tube of paint. She cannot believe she will
have to work to make a color she remembers so clearly. When

she was pregnant she could not eat. Finally, all she could
eat were Granny Smith apples; she was so grateful to be able

to eat those green apples and not throw up. She keeps bowls
of them in her home. They become holy objects, she believes

the baby did not die inside her because she could finally
eat something and it stayed eaten. These apples are not

quite the color green she is searching for. It seems to her
that farmers keep changing the color of Granny Smith apples.

She thinks they are using new chemicals and that the color
and taste are being altered. She does not know where the

beautiful, incredibly soft pale apple-green corduroy dress
is any more. She thinks for a moment she would get pregnant

again if only she could wear that dress again for nine months.
She writes some lines of dialogue for her new novel. The

woman says, "That's the whole point. I hate this cat, but the
cat will die and I'll have to cry and I'll have to bury it

and I won't even have liked the cat and I'll have this whole
set of feelings anyway and that's what I hate." And the man

says, "I don't get it." I never meant to write in the third
person. I woke up one morning and I wanted to start telling

the truth about parts of my life that I never talk about. I
barely believe my life was ever like any of this. It's

unbearably cold today, and yesterday, and the day before
yesterday. My husband's car kind of blew up last Saturday

and I could only laugh. And I read Joyce Johnson's book,
Minor Characters, and got so mad all over again about women

in this culture, women without names, without acknowledgment.
This morning I am thinking about telling the truth and I am

a little cold. There is this path we all think about walking
down toward our future, this path we already walked on. That's

all I can think about, this path, this road that is one perfect
straight line even if it goes around the world through heat

and fog and rain and snow and it's my life I keep thinking.

It's my life.

SECTION II—BURNING

Open Hands

Night comes slow in summer.
There's time to reach your hand
out, time to crouch in the garden,
palm extended to the visiting raccoons.
They lick the tiny marshmallows off
my daughter's palm.

When I see any open hands I think of Christ,
his long walk into death,
its public aspect, his open palms
pierced through to keep him in his place.

My daughter is in her place,
kneeling in the neighbor's backyard,
palms open to wildness,
to hunger and a craving for sweetness.

The night is coming on so slowly
I can see every bloom decide to close.
I can see Christ's hands released, finally,
curve into themselves and rest,
and my daughter's hands finally empty
while the blossoms fade into night's arrival,
and the mother raccoon leads her sated babies
back down the path to wilderness.

Such wilderness He left behind,
going up so slowly the holes in his palms
available to witnesses for only a few
fevered nights, then healed, serene,
opened to the babies, the daughters who kneel
and let the night arrive
without protest.

Alone

Not so bleak today.
She's alone but
not alone.
There are children.
In their early perfection
she sought her image.
Mistakes were made;
she punished herself
over and over again.

The therapist asked her
daughter: Is your mother
needy?

"No."

That was the point.
Be useful or die.

Did her own mother need her?
Yes, but she has a life,
still. Still, the need
holds her in place.

The children are themselves.
Wasn't this the only purpose?
She said, "I don't worry about you,"
to the oldest son, who said,
"I worry about you."

The oldest daughter said:
"She just doesn't get it.
I don't worry. Worry's stupid."

It all feels pretty stupid lately.
Mortal, yes, she's mortal every day
now, staring at her face in the real
mirror.

Her body's alive. She can feel the motor
running down. She doesn't want
to abandon anyone too early, but she might.
Sometimes walking up the stairs she thinks—
now. She doesn't want
to die in any way she can imagine.
She has a large imagination but it's no longer
a comfort to her.

Mothers

The one who begs forgiveness, the one eating the smallest
piece of meat at dinner, uneasy carnivore.

The one lifting the baby to see the moon, the one who helps
the baby see the moon any night without clouds.

She buys the same things at the grocery store each week,
chooses the wrong cereal, redeems herself, reads out loud

past bedtime to the child with tired eyes, the child who
wept, "I said Frosted Flakes, not Corn Pops. Never Corn Pops."

The mother who sees the future, each child adrift, and herself
powerless, the mother playing rock-and-roll songs while children

wait for their turn at the stereo. The mother with too much
to do can't stop listening to STOP MAKING SENSE, the mother

who knows all the words by heart, the mother who doesn't own
her heart too often, the one washing out her son's shirt

by hand after the acrylic paint exploded backwards out of the
tube he held as he bent over his painting, the mother who rages,

who throws the Kirby vacuum cleaner down the stairs, screams
into the beloved child's face, "*I can't do it for you, you must*

care about yourself," the one who's read *Jane Eyre* too many times,
the one looking for privacy, the one who smokes the cigarette,

and the one who's always quitting smoking, the one who's never
lost a child, the one who holds the dying child, and gives her

mind away to the sky, the dirt. The mother cannot let the child die and be called mother, so when the child dies the mother

gives her mind away and does not understand what she is holding in her hands.

Architecture

My father's calling from the bottom of the stairs,
the angry god I've enraged by not picking up
the dish towel fast enough.
Looking down at his face I think I see his vocal cords
drumming inside his throat. Is that my name he's saying?

Looking down he's all face, the roaring mouth,
not god, never god, not king of the garden,
never king of my heart.

In those small moments in his life when sanctimony replaces
vodka, the children are laid on altars, but the prayers
can't go high enough. Then he's despairing, disconnected,
destroyed. There's no vertical energy to his longing.

Up and down the stairs, positions of poverty and power.
I was upstairs, waiting to be summoned, no way out
except down and through what I'd climbed to avoid.

When my brother brought the bottle down on my father's head
and the hallway was bright with glass and blood
I never imagined a straight path through, couldn't see
how to step over his forlorn and broken spirit.

His brilliance never made any light, and oh, the burden
children feel to make light. "I'll be a sunbeam for Jesus,"
and "You are my sunshine, my only sunshine." Do I sing
those songs to my children? Songs full of personal poison,
and these innocent songwriters are clueless as they're inventing,
and these parents, innocent, too,
keep making these neutral and beautiful babies,
and then they keep them.

The Fathers Walking Away From Houses

—For JoAnn Verburg

The fathers walk away from the houses.
We're just girls so maybe we don't see at first
how their shoulders lift, burdens slipping into green
grass, or maybe we notice they walk more smoothly.
The fathers go out side doors or back doors;
they have work to do in the green back yards.

They pick up rakes or trowels; one father
carries new bedding plants meant for shade.
Now he is planting impatiens, now he says,
"Don't be this flower. Don't be impatiens."

Our fathers walk away, and we're girls so maybe
it seems as if they are moving through
a leafy green tunnel, and we already know
they will return to the houses lighter, more lift
in their legs, backs calm and straight.

The fathers walk away from the houses.
The voices of the women and girls don't carry down
the green lawns, and the birds at the crowns
of trees don't speak in feminine song.

We're just girls, and we want our fathers
to be happy. We help them down the steps,
out the door, we tell them, "Walk away
from the house." The fathers carry tools and flowers,
carry green snake hoses and silver buckets.
The fathers do their silent work in the darkening green,
and we tell them, "Come home before night."

Nothing to Eat

—For Rebecca Hill

*"If you want something to eat, go out
and get it, because there's absolutely
nothing to eat in the house."*

The refrigerator was empty because my mother doesn't lie.
In the refrigerator was one white onion.
She cut it open with stainless steel.
She said, "This will help you cry."

She said, "I cut it open for you, my favorite child."
My mother doesn't lie, but her refrigerator was full.

When I walked into the kitchen I opened the white door.
I saw swiss cheese, I saw leaves of lettuce resting
latticed between cool sheets of damp paper towel.
I saw everything that was white and green, so much that
I just wasn't hungry any more.

I love the color green, green for the hearts of trees,
green for new beginnings.
I love the color white. I dress in white to be a bride,
because I am beautiful. I will marry my mother,
my brothers. I will marry the tree in the front yard,
will marry food.

When my brothers get home we will have dinner.
I will eat sparingly because I have seen the poison
in the tall clear jars in my mother's empty refrigerator.

I will watch my brothers eat. Their favorite meal has
been prepared; my mother is waiting for my brothers to come
    home.

I have gone for a walk. I have wrapped my arms around
my best friend.
I left home years ago and live by the rules of the world.
The refrigerator was full but she kept me hungry: now,
when I need food I eat with friends, I wear white, I glance
out any window but I am not looking for my mother.

When The Dead Come to Visit in Dreams

They have questions about placement.
"Where have you assigned me? How many memories are left?"
My father asks if I remember his early beauty.
He asks, "Are you happy?" but is gone before I can think
of the answer he wants, the answer I have.

In the first dream he sleeps in his bed.
My mother sends me in to wake him, I cup my small hand
around the curve of his shoulder, I touch his breathing
waist, I call, "Dad, Dad, it's time to wake up,"
but he sleeps on. I put my mouth to his dreaming ear
and say good-bye.

My mother, standing in the doorframe of the same dream
tells me to take his car and leave. Driving away
in my father's white Studebaker I am so happy. I call
back over my shoulder to say, "Yes, I'm happy,"
then remember the question comes from another dream.

My friend asks if I'm famous, if I've had more children.
When I tell her—another son—she says in her dream voice,
"I hope the new one is quiet. You need some quiet."

When the dead come to visit in dreams they are deeply curious
but disinterested in some holy, unexpected ways.
Most times it doesn't matter what I answer. I can say,
"You're an angel in my sky." I can say, "Dad, I miss you."

I can tell them all this while I'm dreaming, or
on the freeway the next morning, frost past the danger point,
the road a collective illusion. I tell them
I love them. I tell them anything I want.

When the dead come to visit me at night they take some part
of my heart away, as if it's part of some celestial puzzle
they are working on, but they always
bring my heart back to me, and I wake up
lonely, and relieved by their absence.

To Live Without

Certain people die, and then you are done with them,
and they with you.

You have all the stories you are going to get out
of them, you have

all the pathos, all the abuse, all the glorious
kindnesses, you have

whatever it was the two of you made, and unless your
dreams are provocative

and steady, memorable and embedded with new information
that is true

then what I've said is correct. Fathers seem to get more
written for them after

they die. All the poems I've not written about
my dead father

or my living mother. Well, I could start now and never get
done

and I don't feel like it. I can't budge the past
very often.

I can't dream away the fact that I didn't come home for
my father's funeral.

I want to give you the whole scene so you will forgive me,
but nothing has shifted.

I can't make the reasons organized and big. I sent
a bad poem,

a sentimental poem that made people cry who never lived
with my dad. I kept

the lie going in honor of the childhood assignment. I
can be a good daughter

thousands of miles away. I am the best daughter I know
most of the time.

My mother is slipping now, aging faster than I
ever imagined possible,

she is frail, her hands shake. My hands shake, so do the hands
of my oldest

son. From the gene pool these hands rose shaking. I don't
want to write a good-bye

poem to my living mother. I don't want to be filled with
remorse when she leaves.

Fox

I saw a fox, red as a small sunset on cloudless horizon.
Red as flame is supposed to be. It's my childhood

dream: I thought fox traveling fast, fox roaming past
me, intent on his life, thought smaller nose, rounder face,
I thought no teeth, no curled back lip.

When I was small, animals stayed smaller than me. Books
I lived in controlled the dream sizes.

I didn't want to write about the fox dragging the small
rabbit across the road, rabbit dying not dead. It doesn't
matter, one less rabbit. Just another golden book

for the children of foxes. The line of blood was never
in my dream, not that red, not that path.

A friend called to me, said the lop-eared rabbit
in the cage looked like my oldest daughter. "Don't you think
this beautiful rabbit looks like Molly?"

Maybe the eyes, I might have said, the eyes, yes, green
as the weakening forest, no, in the dream it was green
as the wakening forest.

When I was a child no one was telling the story
I ended up living. I was in the forest once. It is so hard
to send my daughters in.

Living

I am living the life of the body one last time with the new
baby. I watch CNN all day and night. When she was brand
new, I watched the beginning of the slaughter in Liberia.
The reporter said, "The victims are mostly women, their heads
taken off, their babies still strapped to their backs.
Dead babies hung from the backs of the dead women.
Many women were murdered in the window frames as they tried
to escape from the church they'd gone to for sanctuary."

Today my safe white body smelled of milk and pizza. My oldest
son wept in my arms; he'd just come off a twelve hour shift
driving the pizza truck. If a friend calls, I ask what day
it is. My oldest son says, "They'll never catch me, mom. And
they say you can come home after seven years." I think of
Tranströmer, the grass whispering amnesty, how many years I've
carried the poem in my heart. My heart pounds and wakes the
baby.

Liberia was created by Africans who so despised their lives of
slavery in America they returned across the ocean to be free.
It is months later now; today's weather report says heavy fog
in St. Paul, heavy fog in Baghdad. Regular human beings are
praying and singing, regular human beings have been carrying
candles and praying for peace.

My little son has learned to move through the neighborhood
without me. He has crossed his first streets, his first alleys
without me. When we brought the baby home Joey looked huge,
I sat and tried to remember the size of his skull when he
was born, but now his head looked enormous, almost mutant.
His perfect eyes seemed too large. His beautiful arms and legs

35

giant appendages, inappropriate and looming next to Cordelia's immense smallness. My mother says, "Don't you just love a baby's hands?" Yes, I do.

Here in the world I feel crazy possessing a regular life. My oldest son says, "Who are the four people who will write my letters, saying my way has always been the way of peace?" A year ago I let my cynical nature slip, wept as the wall went down. Now the new baby is a few months old. My four children came from my body loving peace, but I cannot protect them with the war stories that invade my poems.

Wrong

In the face of all that is wrong in the world,
In the face of all that's wrong within,

In the walk each day that each day calms,
But only for that day, small hour claimed by thievery,

In the swamps of good intention, in the leaps of faith
Between one day, into its night, to the breaking sky

That carries us forward, how I heard your voice
At the door, demanding, "Let me out to see the sunrise,"

How I came quickly, lifting you higher than my arms
Believed, carried you to the middle of the empty street,

How you crooned at the plum streaks, the violent pinks,
How you applauded beauty, tiny hands pressing

Together on the black street, in the way we walked
Back to the door, you, captured by beauty for another

Morning, me, pale as the lamplight that greeted us, that gave
Us a circle to read in, how the wrongness of the world

Stepped outside the diameter of the circle, how the wrong
Inside and outside abated, and we opened the book, read

The words, "Come to the window my baby with me, and look
At the stars that shine on the sea," how we talked and

I said, "There is no sea," and you told me I was wrong
As we left the light to stand at the square window,

How you leaned away from my body to show me the blue
Sea in the sky, with waves of gray and gold.

37

Burning

"Control nature," my father said.
Or: "We must get this yard under control."
I think that's right.

I thought of myself as doing the best I could.
Filling buckets, carrying them, aching fingers
coiled around metal, down the slope,
one bucket for each new tomato plant.
I first made a moat for each green life.
I tilted the lip of the bucket
and the moats filled. I watched the stalks lift,
the green veins fill.

Now there's other conversation.
My son says, "Could you do that in the olden days?"
And I say, "Yes, we could burn and burn and no one cared."
What city friends never understand—not just the leaves
of autumn burned, but in March and April we burned
a line across the back acres, getting rid
of last year's stubble, burning the volunteers
my father hadn't planted himself.

Now I know I was too young to be left
in charge of a line of fire. Where did he go
that spring day, leaving me with a rake,
a hose that didn't stretch far enough?

I think he went for a drink, a bottle hidden
in the rose bushes, or maybe for another nap of oblivion;
then I only felt he'd given me a precious job.
I don't remember feeling small until the fire jumped
in the wind, and my rake, my anxious movements couldn't hold
the heat in place.

It doesn't matter. The yard survived, though fire took
the raspberry patch, three pines, the best oak for climbing.

I see my son and daughter think I'm old, a pioneer
who believed in burning for free, a sky that could abide
smoke and forever be clean.

The yard's rearranged now. One tornado, two straight line
wind storms, two brothers, one girl, handy neighbors
carrying spring promises. The willows my father planted
still grow in the next yard, land sold off
when his job was taken from him.
He controlled nothing, finally, but the patient
and decisive movement of his body into the path
of a train.

What jobs are right for children?
I give my daughter no line of fire
to guard. I ask too little, I think,
and worry they will never be serious enough
for the world.

I stand now under the willows, knowing they root faster,
grow farther, lift higher than any other tree I might choose
for my plot of city land. My father said,

"You plant a willow, and you'll still be around
to see it tower over you."

SECTION III—HAPPINESS

Happiness

*"I could say it's the happiest period of my life.
It hasn't got much competition!"*
                            —John Ashbery

I.

Woke this morning, tropical wind. Hawaii all those years ago,
trade winds carrying rain to the small Waikiki jungle where

I walked with my first baby boy. Was I unhappy? I look
at the pictures. Pictures lie so much. Bread crumb clues

birds swoop to eat. Hansel, Gretel, no way home. That was
part of it. In the real story it's not step-mother but real

mother. The real mother says, "There's not enough food for
all of us." The real father does her bidding, remember?

In Hawaii I loved the wind. Years later did I draw a black
line around time that I owned, and make the decision for

silence? When I read Ashbery's poem I wondered if I was
happy enough to understand my happiness, or sad enough,

or is it just trying to make it through the winter one more
time, years later, and there's the handwritten note from

Charlie, lunch with friends, my list of grief competing with
every menu. Do I get to have my friend? That's what I

meant to ask David. Are you leaving because one day, no
matter what I do, my skin will look too white and devilish

for you to abide? There were so many things to ask, and we
got through a lot of them, so I let my heart lighten up;

that's the truth. We had a jeep in Hawaii that I didn't
drive because I didn't learn, but why? And walking to the

library along the canal, Brendan in the stroller, the native
boy riding his bike toward me at a speed I refused to

acknowledge, his fist a flag, his arm extended in rage.
Was it rage? My white skin, extended, and his fist smashing

into my left breast, I remember surprise that the blow
didn't drag him from his bike, just this huge purple, turn

to black, turn to green, turn to yellow, turn to white again
bruise covering a whole white breast. My body. I guess I

was thinking this morning I am glad I wasn't nursing my
little boy, then it would have been more of a violation.

And people touching people in elevators, and people saying,
"White people hate being too close, hate their skin touching,"

and I think about my color every day, I guess partly this is
surprise. That I had to say it. That I will never know what it

means to be not white/devilish/white/ghostly. In church we
sit close. In elevators, that's right, I don't like strangers

too close to my body. "I could say it's the happiest period
of my life," but I won't. So many things are just a trick

of language or privilege, to walk by canals so far from home,
"Oh, holy southern cross," James Taylor sang yesterday when

I was white and happy for about half an hour.

II.

I start with small demands. Seven neighbors in a row who will
mow their lawns, plant a few flowers, petunias, marigolds—order.

But the walking makes me want more. That's the way desire for
order corrodes the spiritual journey. The mother shrieking

in a voice that scares and wants to scare, the red-faced
father shouting from his truck, elbow cutting into the street,

"Just stay home, then, be the sissy I always knew you were,"
his son weeping on the back stoop, the chocolate-colored dog

lapping water, not comforting the boy at all. I admit I don't
want to hear it, don't want to see it either. I want to be

good but I want the world to help me and it won't. I can't
rush into people's houses where voices are breaking a perfectly

good sunset with crazy anger, can't pick up any-sized child
and walk out their front door saying, "You can't have this

child back until . . ." Then I stop loving the sunset that a
minute ago meant everything to me, I can't even see how the

purple and orange go together splendidly, correctly, I don't want
to know about the gray clouds that make the whole sky work

just by being gray clouds. I lose my smallness, my sense of
my small place on the planet. I work hard in my mind just to

be able to see the lawns again, I imagine knocking on a door,
saying, "Your garden is really working this year, I like your

new sprinkler, I like how the grape ivy is finally wrapping
around your porch like I bet you wanted it to grow last year

but it wouldn't." I know you can't do this kind of stuff without
the neighborhood tumbling down around you. "Intervene,

intervene," the moon calls to me now, but it doesn't mean it.
The moon is just moon and borrowed light and shape. I am

supposed to look at it right now so I do. And it works. I am
looking at something that does its job right.

III.

Knowing paradise doesn't mean you can stay. And, my father
said, "Earn your luck." The yard is full of wild animals turning

tame. The badgers' stripes are distinctive, not like the skunks'
pure white line when my flashlight hits, and the deer lift

their tails to run and that's white too, and the moles and the
pocket gophers rarely surface, but my mother cries and pounds

on their tunnels with an old iron shovel, and she screams down
their holes, "Stay out of our yard," and my father calls it

"my yard," and I call it "my yard," and my brothers call it
"our yard," but the moles and pocket gophers and the raccoons

don't call it anything, just own it when we're not around to
stop them. Is it paradise? It was sort of paradise, I answer,

lots of graves for all the creatures who died in our yard, or
in the woods across the street. I'd carry anything dead home.

Graves for the kittens who didn't survive, and for all my
brother's golden dogs, dead by poison or drowning, and stealing

pieces of my mother's velvet I'd wrap the small bodies, and if
they'd been ripped apart by another wild animal I'd try to wrap

them tight so their bodies would fit back together. In heaven
they'd be whole, my mother said, but I wanted to help. So,

it was paradise, I guess, because so many animals left for
heaven from our three acres it felt like a way-station to God.

I was afraid of the raccoons even though the neighbors fed them
like children; their claws were sharp and shapely, I could hear

them fit their claws under the tight lids of our garbage cans
and the sound of metal circling, circling on cement as it rang

down to silence and they began their midnight feast. I thought
they were too smart, and that they would climb the walls of my

gray house and maybe they would talk to me but probably not,
probably they would kill me, so story books didn't work that

had raccoons in them. But the badgers would waddle and travel
in their family groups, and that was fine with me, and all

the creatures were fine with me, really. I loved how real
they were, and when I slept outside in the summer I felt them

circled around me as if I were a fire for them, as if I were
the center of something wild. "*I could say it's the happiest*

period of my life." My brothers climbed to the top of the
Linden tree, they saw the first skyscraper go up in the city

down the road, they called down to me to come up, but I froze
on the bottom limb, I was sick, and they called to me to come

and see the city but I couldn't move. Paradise was on the ground.
I didn't want a big view with too much sky showing. They left

to go to college, doing what they were supposed to do, but
paradise was over by then, and I threw the tennis ball by my-

self every night, spinning white into the night sky, higher
and higher and I'd clap my hands as many times as I could before

catching it; how good did I get at this game? I was very good
at the game, and when they came home to visit we would play

catch and every caught ball meant a step backwards, and we were
very good at this game too, my palms stung for a week after

they left for all the colleges they ended up leaving for, and
I missed my brothers, and wrote them letters, and they were

brothers from paradise and always wrote back to me, their little
sister left behind.

IV.

The children were born and it wasn't a dream. Summer came
and the heat made me dull with happiness. Only in summer

could I feel my heart beat with a measured slowness, could
I slow down the brain waves pounding "should," "should,"

and "do more," "do more," pounding "not enough, never
    enough."
Who wouldn't cry when summer ended? I was glad to cry at

the end of summer's happiness, reach for work, money, sorrow,
reach for the schedules that might break the family's happiness:

48

mother, father, sons, daughter—who had been happy, all of them,
because the sun wore them down to happiness—but were already

giving up the memory, even on the September day that recalled
summer, you could hear their voices, nostalgic for themselves,

the slow people they'd been, what was gone now recorded in
every golden glade of leaves, every leaf on fire that brushed

their faces in flight. We were saying good-bye, we were settled into
our new unhappiness, calm with autumn headaches and fears.

I wanted to stop the summer from leaving. I wanted to admit
my complicity, the deals I make with work and sorrow, how I

gamble for happiness every year, telling the devil or God
I'll be good or I'll be bad if I can just have that slowness

of summer one more time; it's all about wanting to leave
things behind, sisters and fathers, seasons and hot memories.

That was why I started the poem, "Happiness." In my dream I
am searching for my daughter, the dream is all tone and

highway, no color, no characters. I know my daughter is lost
and in the dream I can tell it is already too late. I've

read the map wrong, I'm too late, though I drive the road,
though I run, I cannot stop her from dying. I think of this

dream in summer, how slow I am though my heart is pounding
with love and terror, I'm too slow, I think, this dream

is poison to my love for summer. If I slow down I will lose her.
Not "lose her." That she will die because I am slow.

In gold leaves yesterday I felt my happiness like a stone in
my hands, a treasure not too heavy to carry. I carried the

stone under the ceiling of leaves, outdoor room of butter and
copper, the stone clicking against my wedding ring, my rings

from the ocean, my father's ring. Clicking and slipping
slightly inside my curled fingers. I was warm and I knew

my daughter was alive at home, curled in a position of safety
and sleep. Daughters die, I thought, carrying the stone.

Friends have lost daughters to death. And there's the terrible
cry that comes to my throat in the dream: not my daughter,

not this one. In the dream the cry feels primal and correct;
remembering it in light I feel white, middle-class, puny-

voiced. Not my daughter, I scream, and the voice is white in
the yellow air, then I pause in the forest and roar it louder,

my voice mixes with the butter and copper, with the hidden
deer who breathe around me, I scream it louder and lower,

the hook of my breath is low in my body, now I don't sound
white or black or golden or brown, I sound like a mother,

a walking mother in the forest, roaring out a boundary to a
dream-maker she's always believed was someone else, not her.

v.

My oldest son explains that everything is balanced. If I mention
news from Poland or Romania, if an optimistic phrase comes from

my cynical mouth, he quickly reminds me of tyrants elsewhere,
or the rain forests falling in honor of money; he explains

it all to me; for every kind action on our block, a cruel word
rocks a classroom, for every child saved there's a child

dead or worse than dead. Then my little son mentions that most
people die because they are old, but Martin Luther King, Jr.

died of a gun. He says, "I guess he won't be the only one," he
says, "Do you get to pick which way you want to die?" Everything

feels very balanced to me now, and the balance immobilizes.
If I say "peace" someone says "war" and cancels me out. If I

love the new baby we will have when summer finally comes,
some other summer child will be purely hated, perfectly damaged.

The children are playing Opposites. Cross-legged they stamp
closed fists onto their legs twice, click their fingers twice,

one child says, "hot," not losing the rhythm, the child next in
the circle says "cold," and the game goes smoothly until my

child says "turquoise" and the circle blows apart. The other
children are furious, she has ruined the game, has said a word

for which there is no opposite, and now there is no more balance.
The game is over. Did she know how powerful she was?

I hold her in my arms; it is hours later. She's not crying. She
hardly ever cries. She explains to me that she always thought

turquoise's opposite was magenta. I see what she means. I mean,
I see what she means. We get the crayons out. We color the rest

of the day away. She says, "Somebody always gets mad. That's
why circle games don't ever ever ever ever work." We can't

color any more. It is night. We have colored so many flowers,
so many animals, trees, dinosaurs. We are all very tired.

VI.

Hard to learn that happiness is a talent, like any other.
That you can practice it, woo it, ignore it, despise it.

I think my brothers and I have a talent for happiness.
I think of my father in his garden, my mother in her dancing

dresses, the bloody velvet of his roses, the scratch
and edge of her green taffeta. In the old days our house

smelled of Camel cigarettes and cocktails the color of warm
jewels. I loved the smell, lying on my single bed, my little

transistor radio connected to me by a tiny ear plug, a yard
of transmitting wire, I listened to folk singers and pretended

I was my deaf grandmother. My antique dolls studied me gravely,
their goat kid bodies odorless and white, their porcelain faces,

tiny white teeth showing between rose-painted lips. How to learn
happiness in the house of childhood? We were all so bad at it,

so often, "I could say it's the happiest period of my life" but
it wasn't. I don't think I was interested in happiness then,

the animals I watched in the backyard woods weren't looking for
happiness, my expensive dolls were calm, not happy, I just wanted

to be in it, that's how I remember my early years, I just wanted
it, life, surrounding me and bowling me over like a wild wave at

Jones Beach that one summer visit, I just wanted to wake up in my
sleeping bag and look up into the face of a deer, I wanted to

light fires and ride my white bike so far and fast no one could
imagine I would ever come back. Inside the snow house that one

winter it was so white and silent. I lived in a white world, and
when Frank sent us *National Geographic* I remember staring at all

the colors people could be and feeling like a slab of snow, pale
and somehow not well, as if I was the sickly child in an old-

fashioned story book, the child who always died, white and dead
and good, who made the regular children cry and promise to be

good, too. I was hungry and timid, a creeping white cat, but
finally too hungry to stay so safe. Only in my bravery did I

interest myself. And I am brave less and less often now. My
children are brave. I remember Gary saying to me, years ago,

that my mother would send him out into the world with my
brothers whether it was a journey, or college, love or work, she

would say, "Go, just make sure you come back and tell me about
it." He loved her for that, called her a remarkable word

I've forgotten, let me see how she sent others out on voyages,
gave her blessing to disappearances and fears and bravery.

My children are brave and I'm not any more. I fear that
I convinced them so long ago how much trouble the world

is in that they grew up feeling they weren't allowed to want
happiness. I call them to me—it's another kind of balance

I want to explain to them. This happiness that is so much work
and so much luck. I have said good-bye to my children for years.

I practiced, not wanting to be caught unawares when they left
at seventeen or eighteen to own their lives more completely.

I think I made them feel a great distance. I think sometimes
they wondered if I loved them every day. I just wanted them to

know they could leave, that they would be strong and safe without
me. Sometime maybe one will say to me that I disappeared,

abandoned them to their freedom long before they wanted it. I
don't know many things. In the middle of the country on a

cold day in February I think of my brothers, alive by each ocean,
my father, confined to his small space in the graveyard, my

mother, still honoring happiness in our family home, the deer
still coming to the back windows, huge brown eyes of wildness

staring at her sewing basket, her decks of cards, the walls
covered with photographs of the living and the dead. The deer

turn away, they've seen all this before, they are more gray
than brown this late in the winter, they have used up most

of their winter weight. Lean and on their guard they leap away
to their lives in the woods. The moon lives on their bodies.

SECTION IV—WHAT DRIVES US

What Drives Us

*"The force that grows
in Napoleon's dreams
and tells him to conquer Russia
is also in poems
but is very still."*
　　　　　—Adam Zagajewski

Not still enough in too many voices.
I'm on the watch for the bitter edge,
the poets of promise who used to like writing.

Jean Simmons was Desiree, Brando, Napoleon,
and as a girl the movie made me shake though
I did not understand it was desire.

There's this trick of the culture, or else
girls' genetics don't convince them that
conquering countries matters. We stay at home

waiting for some Napoleon, or one of his guards,
to spring through the window with lilacs
to toss on the bridal bed, we open to cross the body's

border, but we don't want to own Italy, we don't
want to write the poem that makes all other poems
meaningless. Why don't we want this?

Poets in translation always sound so intelligent,
as if a small Buddha has perched on their shoulders
since infancy guiding them away from competition,

depravity, pettiness, ownership. The desire to be
the only one. Poets in translation so consistently sound
right I've come to mistrust their beautiful voices.

The force in Napoleon's dreams propels poems I read
in my native tongue, invasions against any absence
of bitterness, against a yearning to be still.

Loving Motels

Feels American.
Shameless, somehow.
People I don't know
love motels. People
I don't know love chlorine;
hundreds and thousands of people
I know and don't know
love motel pools, whirlpools,
hot tubs, saunas.
People I love, people who love
me, those people love room service.
The sheer
intellectual weight: the idea of a phone,
wires, another phone, then food arriving.
Preposterous and sexual.
Sexy, like those bathing suits
you only wear in pools
in motels in Montreal, or
pools in Shawnee Mission, any pool
where no one you know will walk by
and know you.
Loving motels means loving
what has not rooted in your spirit.
Loving motels is loving
your very own ice bucket,
and the special shapes the ice takes,
is loving the shining cans of pop
sinking through the melting ice,
the sound aluminum makes
while you pretend to sleep,
is loving the hidden air conditioners
and the cable TV shows, and is
letting no one else, not even someone

you love, use your own wrapped
bar of soap, or your own little pack
of ten-month-old Sanka
or the sweet little hot plate
that just fits the baby coffee pot.
People like me and including me
love motels for the white towels
which remind us of something large
we have lost somewhere. We love
the deep shag carpet we would hate
at home. We love the key,
the number, the simple locks,
not like home where locks are hard,
needing a hip thrown against
the door, the dead bolt really dead,
we love the simple key with the simple
plastic shape: sometimes a fish,
sometimes a smooth, beige oval,
sometimes, if we're lucky,
a shamrock, a clover, a doll or dog.
We love motels for letting us
drive up, we get our own parking place
automatically, then we get love-
making that is not connected
to our own bed's history,
and besides the white towels
we get white sheets
which we all love and never buy.
We get left alone,
we get the feeling of being alone,
and we need America to leave us
alone in the motels.

The Fish Bowl

"I love this fish bowl, but will the
fish live without a bubble machine?"

"That's the big question . . ."

I've hated fish all my life; I've never been drawn to
their lack of eyelids, their dramatic lifestyles.

I don't look back with fondness of false memory
to the small fish biting me in the lakes of my childhood,

I've never eaten a fish I wouldn't rather have not eaten.

During years I lived alone with my oldest children,
desperate to be a glorious mother across all the lines of
interests, passions, loathings, my son begged for a fishing
rod, a tackle box, became obsessed with flies and lures,
I lived in hardware stores for one summer, learning about
single hooks, quadruple hooks, about the intentions of fishermen.

Once he caught a fish in my mother's creek. The fish was
caught in four ways and I ran through the park, the rod
in my hand, yelling for help as the fish flew through the air
at my side, stunned with air and pain.

Now my friends have given their little son a fish bowl, and one
little fish to go with it. I admire my friends for allowing
a creature not a mammal into their lives. I love the stones
in the bottom of the bowl, brilliant blue, and the seaweed
is blue too, like turquoise mixed with sky mixed with the holy
blue color of Renaissance paintings. The blue is transfixing.

The fish swims lazily in a blue world. In plain water. Andre
loves the bowl, loves the fish. I love the blue, only, but
for one moment wonder how this fish can survive with so much
love and no fish tank apparatus. Must the fish live until
the boy is bored with him; must the boy love the fish to keep
the fish alive?

What Went Wrong at the Beach

—for Charlie Baxter

Nothing. That's the problem with the beach.
The ocean was a home, the water warm from the last hurricane.

Destruction elsewhere means fine swimming.
And I swam. The problem with the beach is how little
it is like real life. When you put your foot down

in the sand you are on the ground. The sand sends accurate
messages: Yes, I'm hot today. Put on your tennis shoes.
Yes, I'm cool from last night's rain. Build your castle quickly.

A friend said, "Don't you understand? You are on the ground
floor of your character. Even when you say you're feeling crazy
you're sane because you're not up in the scaffolding, knowing
if you try to step to the ground floor you might die,
you might change, you might die."

She didn't say it exactly like that. I made a little poetry
out of it, and that's what's wrong with not being at the beach.

At the beach, hardly anything is poetry. Being inarticulate
in the face of waves and sand is the correct and holy posture.
But she's right. I'm not on the scaffolding on my character.
My job is moving from friend to friend with a net; then my
job is remembering my net doesn't matter. It's a lot of work
and often not a pretty sight.

What went wrong at the beach was leaving it.
This is the smallest lie I've ever told, a lie I can live with.

The City

I've come to love the skyline at least;
it's not always kind like a perfect friend,
but it's beautiful, and lit.

I want to know what I'm getting into,
and the city's clear, at least. There's the building
I belong in to pay the rent, and another
where I could steal books but don't.

Driving into the city, my foot doesn't err,
now I know how much gas for the curve,
how to touch the brake just so
and find my way, though the buildings
are, at this very moment, so full
of the breaking light of sunrise I am blinded
by the beauty.

Even when using electricity was a crime
in the minds of left-wing America
I still voted for lighting the edges of everything.

I wrapped the lines of my house in Christmas colors,
I judged the skyline at night, loving the squandered
white and golden lights defining the skyscrapers.

I am alone in my car. I don't think I've ever
taken a ride with a perfect friend,
talk is just talk most of the time
and I'd rather have the music pound into me
than just about any speaking voice.

Music's not so kind either. Each song places
me in my past, like a shoehorn, or a slap
or an erotic tremor.

When I can't bear the song
I punch on the news,
when I can't bear the news
I listen to my heater go through its stages
of warmth and cooling.

I don't want my love to go any farther than this;
I don't want to love light any more than I do,
I want it to end this way, the buildings on fire
with light; not loving the city is my choice.

Condor

——"Should we grant reprieve to the condor?
——No, we won't grant reprieve to the condor.
It didn't eat from the tree of Knowledge
and so it must perish."
——Czeslaw Milosz

The fox, too, must die. Foolish in his red coat,
sly and so selfish. How dare he live and eat the innocent?

And the wolf. We believe none of the research. Fairy tales
tell the truth, so bring the axes quickly, quickly before
the wolf finds one more advocate.
Burn those calendars. Especially May, the gentle cubs
are seductive; children cry out for them.

The raccoon in the attic. Kill her, too. She's got babies
inside, and clever claws,
and no sense of dignity.

The carp deserve the spears;
the boys cry out with power as blood
glows in the creek.

The tree grows at the edge of the creek.
Nourished by the stained water its branches
disarm the wind as it blows.

It is still in the forest,
and we believe we are famished.
No part of the tree offers itself to us,
no part of the tree appeals to our hunger.

The animals gather as twilight discharges
its last useless beauty before darkness.

Rogue Wave

In Miami, that exotic
land, the Rogue Wave
came from nowhere
the meteorologists
swear, nowhere,
traveled seventy-five
feet without effort
crossing the boundary
of beach, of good taste,
of rules the tourists
thought they were living
by. That wave came
at night, wise wave
full of water smarts
and didn't carry away
any moon bathers, just
swept a three-year-old's
hand from her mother's
while they were
standing outside
a convenience store
at 11:30 at night,
and the mother said
something like, I just
planted my feet and
opened my arms as wide
as I could and prayed
the wave was on a straight
path and would bring
my child back to me.
And the wave in its
kindness did return
the child alive,

brought the child
with force and precision
into the open body
of the mother.
The Rogue Wave took
several kiosks out
to sea, and many
racks of T-shirts,
and hundreds of pairs
of plastic thongs
which later sharks
with bad eyesight
thought were small
neon-colored carp.
The Rogue Wave
complicated so
few lives that
it has been forgotten
except by
the mother, who swims
now each day, who
never liked the water
before it gave
back her daughter,
except by
the daughter, who churns
in her blankets each night,
swept away, over
and over again,
panicked and lost,
free, then held
by human arms.

Why They Belong Together

In this cemetery coyotes and jackals mate. Their babies glisten
in full summer sun. I am not afraid of these helpless babies,
only their parents, teeth full of moonlight.

Buddha, so huge in your peacefulness. I could not pray
to anyone so untormented. Your dreams are simple; you do not
even fall asleep to have them.

I believe in justice, struggle to commit more than good manners
and my children's upbringing to that slippery word.

The Buddha doesn't care, but he's clear about that. I would fly
past him in a helicopter. I would touch his golden face with
my human hand. I would give him anything.

In the graveyard I cannot find the few stones I am searching for.
When my mother dies, I am to move my father's ashes to her grave
in Salt Lake City. The lawyer said, "Plan ahead. You need three
separate permits to move him." I told him my father has always
been lots of work, but I've had years of rest. The only real
question is: will either of them know if I don't do my job?

My baby's arms are outstretched with passion toward the dog
coming down the street toward us. Clearly he could take her face
off before I could stop him, but she offers herself up, her face
a pond for every dog she embraces.

Right now, the idea of sunlight seems foreign, as if the sun
never sent me into rapture.

Buddha, my hand touches your left eye, and there is still room
for many other hands before we could block your sight, halfway.
But I am by myself, in natural light, and I suddenly do not want
to touch you at all.

The World

The sex of the world
is never hidden.

This is a problem in the world.
Magic said, "I accommodated as many ladies
as I could . . . there are certain
sexually desirable people.
There is a list. We can get it
any time we wish." And we wish it

constantly.
When do we see
when we see the world?
Trees and flowers and skyscrapers
opening and closing.
A sexual mouth opens and closes,
flower with no season.
The mouth of the fish
risking everything.

In the eye
of the storm we are sexual people,
sexual animals, sexual plants
sucked into the terror of the wind.
The world grows quiet then,
and the dead tumble from the sky.

What can we do with this openness?
Desire, the wound we carry,
is open.

The Red Fox / Truro

—For Peggy Dillon

In morning light the walk
down Old King's Highway is not moody
or surprising.

Light of morning breaks into each secret glen,
the twisted, bankrupt oaks scrub against
each other, and the juniper and milkweed
stay low, dense, and recognizable.

At dusk the ancient highway pulls away
from its summer visitors, demands its own
pilgrim and pirate history.
We're not as welcome at twilight
as each of us walks in one of two grooves
made centuries ago by wagon wheels,
each rutted path a distinct shade of old sand,
one, nearly white, one, nearly gold.

Before the plunge down the steepest hill
Peggy and I stare at the serene and darkening
horizon, eyes watching for the sun nesting down
in the bayside water, eyes looking to the ocean side.
We can feel the forest coming alive, we are the last
humans before night, when the animals
take to the highway.

I look down the white hill, the fox
is standing there, red and wild
as myth and menace, and I say, "What is that?"

I've asked myself over and over, now
that I've left the ocean behind for another year,
and of course it was a fox, though city eyes
don't know much worth knowing
in the forest of summer walks.

She and I agree it is a fox, though
fox for us could be wolf, could be dog, could
be anything we don't know, don't trust.
We say "fox" outloud, suppose he'll run
at the one syllable announcement of his human name,
and he does, straight toward us.

Peggy takes a stick, cracks it over her knee,
hands me half, the way we might share
the last piece of fudge from Provincetown,
the last ear of corn; she and I know
how to share the humblest of objects,
we know everything we need to know, it seems,
except how to recognize a fox,
or scare it away.

I decide to pretend I must pass the fox
in order to save all the children,
my four, her two, the six who wait
in the dark house. Peggy may choose
her own bravada fantasy, but we still can't believe
the fox won't turn away from us.

He holds our eyes, keeps our bodies still,
then ten feet away he stops, not for fear
of women warriors, but because his ears
hear the steady steps of a summer jogger
coming up the hill behind us.

As the man passes the fox pivots, leaps
into the dirty air of almost night, white sand
spitting under his turning paws, and the red fox
runs into the forest as the jogger thuds
down the hill.

We ask him something about the red fox
as he passes us, we ask him if we should be afraid,
though there's no "should" in the adrenalin
we've bathed ourselves in, and he says, "red fox, yes,
they live here," and he says, "don't be afraid," and he turns
on the next hill, looks back at us still waiting
on the crown of the hill, carrying our oak weapons,
and he says, delightedly, "is that what your sticks are for?"

Peggy and I walk home. Toss our sticks
into the jumble of underbrush, laugh wild whoops
of laughter; then we're very quiet.
We talk about who owns what, and why, we talk
about pointed ears and shades of red,
we talk about what we're afraid of, and
the list is comprehensive, natural, and long.

SECTION V—WHAT IT WAS LIKE TODAY

Comfort

*"We have everything we need to believe
right here in front of us."*
—Dabney Stuart

I put my mouth on the wound of the tree.
I breathed, a child in my father's yard.
My breath was a Valentine, came from my red heart.

The tree lived long past the time of its wound.
My father went to his grave, and I believed in his death.
In the yard I would do his work, taught my children his name.

My mother inside the window watched us
and we turned to wave, her love for us involuntary,
streaming through the glass; she held her position.

My oldest son said, high in the branches of the tree,
"Here are his arms, I am swinging from his arms."
The tree turned to me, promised to live until I could do

without him.

What It Was Like Today

I was studying at the dining room table and looked out the front window. Saw my car parked on the street, metal proof I was home. Reading Audre Lorde, reading Frank O'Hara, taking too many notes.

The other night my oldest son was awake half the night though I did not know it until morning. He'd been afraid to call out to us for fear of waking his baby brother, and afraid to leave his room because in his dream the werewolves were at his door, and he had seen another one perched on his window sill. He had a long night, though I heard him laughing about it with a friend soon enough. This morning, driving him to school, he said, "white people" with such disgust I burst out laughing. We had been talking about Martin Luther King, about how much history I'd lived through.

Today, when I saw my car on the street I admitted I was part of history, that I was positioned, that my heart was home, that my children's hearts were at that very moment beating in three different places, white children, and I thought of my daughter making a Martin Luther King board game for an assignment. Playing the game with her stepdad one night I heard him laugh because he got ten points for knowing the first name of King's first child, but only four points for knowing where King delivered his "I Have A Dream" speech. I listened to him try to explain that it was what King did that mattered more than the name of his child, so he thought her point system was flawed.

Last night all my children died in a specific way in my dream. Around four A.M. the war I keep waiting for finally arrived and I was sitting on our old couch which my son insults each day, the dreadful brocade pattern, the hideous green and turquoise colors, and somehow I was holding all three of them in my arms, watching TV in some dreadful parody of the ways we watch TV, listening to the announcement that the bombs were flying, were falling, and as I sat there each child turned to vapor, turned to dust and ash in my arms, and I remember thinking in my dream that it was terrible to be holding something substantial, like flesh, like the silken feel of children's skin, or the feel of the baby's corduroy overalls against my wrist, and then to feel my children as dust, utterly dry, the beautiful blood absent, the liquid eyes dust, their three differently shaped mouths dust, their Dr. Who T-shirts dust, I remember thinking: where are they? and in the dream I wept to be left alive, sitting on the damn couch trying to get their dust off my hands, the texture was like cleaning the vacuum cleaner, dirty and absolutely dry, and then I woke and thought of snow never falling, rain never falling, tears never falling, thought of each child having one bath a day, needing all that water, thought of water fountains in three schools, thought of them.

I was grateful to wake from my dream, but today I am sick of myself in some special way, ashamed that I let my children go to their schools, that I did not answer the power of the dream by keeping their warm flesh and blood around me today, but I didn't keep them home, and I will not sit on the couch with all three of them again for a long, long time, the long long time I want to be their lives, not all four of us on the couch, not for a long and dreamless time.

Lilacs and Hail

—For Cheryl Miller and Will Powers

The air's midwestern. There's this one perfect
month. First forsythia breaks open along the bark,
yellow petals shaped like small mussel shells, and
then the lilacs begin, first the ordinary lavender,
drenching the air with sweetness, then two days later
the white lilacs that brides and children sleep with.

A pause, and then the French lilac opens, and then
it just stays. That's what we meant to write you.
We tore armfuls from the tree, and it never showed,
and the scent was lyric, from the middle of the country.

Before the bridal's wreath in its curves, before the
sand cherry tree with its starlight blossoms, during
the wild flowering of the crabapple trees, that's when
the hail fell from the sky, and our street was a steel
drum band, each car hood a different pitch depending
on the quality of the tin, or the quality of the hail.

We came out of our houses. The earth is so dry here, and
the hail stones melted into the green lawns so quickly,
like a hard worker racing through dinner, like the grass
needed the hail to hold onto its green, so the hail came
like music and everyone was laughing. Then the sky
cleared, two rainbows jazzed up the sky, people got shier
and left their front porches.

The air's so sweet. There's one month when the possibility
of paradise seems to live in every alley, and the Hmong kids
and the black kids and the white kids are playing
basketball, and their spring jackets decorate
the lilac trees, and we fall asleep to the sound of the
basketballs bouncing in the alley, to the sound of the hoop
letting the ball fall in the scent of the night.

Against the Good

Who can vote against the good?
The easy and expected beauty:
you know the list: ocean, lily,
throat of a swan.

I'm in a dream now.
Nothing fearful or ugly comes
my way, so waking holds few
rewards this morning.

Today I will think about
things you never brought me:
unfolding flowers that captivated,
peace that was a willingness
for days to be
ordinary but all right.

I think that you always
voted against the good.
And your unhappiness,
your commitment to all
that was broken and wrong
filled me with sorrow
I now see as rage. So
I feel the rage like a
natural force: house-smashing
wind, sun at the equator.
I'm useless now, passionate
yet changing nothing.

Night Walk

The last lover you had before your first marriage
called a few weeks ago.
You felt the heat.
When he asked about old friends you'd known
in common you said, "Being with you, all I remember
is a dark circle; we didn't even have each other
in common."

That interested him, neither of you moonlight
for the other; you could read his swift intake of breath
over the wires.

He said, "I think we must live near each other. The phone
caught so quickly, the ring, I mean."

You thought of voodoo, his pale blue eyes,
sixteen years of silence.

And then you started running, not walking,
and a girl stood on the hood of her car at Hamline and Summit
screaming, "Don't hurt my car, you assholes."
Holding a ray-gun, a pitchfork in her hand.

You started running because people are frightening,
except for kind lovers, or your husband, "the kindest man
who ever loved you."

Your old lover lives close by, you'd assumed him dead
in Central America, underground in D.C., but you have
walked past his house for two years now without knowing.

Now you avoid his street, the simple code of his address.
Who can you live with in a circle of light?

A car goes by and you believe the silver bike
tied to the top is a Christmas tree.
You haven't even noticed the moon,
though it hangs, a perfect circle in the sky.

You see two lovers embracing near the stand of crabapple trees.
You feel huge as you run past them, bodiless and gigantic
with your double shadow.

You're close to home now; the moon becomes real.
Your lover said, "I guess we'll see each other
when we're supposed to."

The phone is light in your hands,
nothing is casual enough.

This lover was disembodied for so long,
the myth you never put down,
how he died in Nicaragua,
how the ashes blew your way,
and you caught his hand, his heart.

You told your friend this week,
"Let the young man go who killed himself.
You slow him down by thinking his light
is still around. You slow down his journey
with your anger. Let him go to heaven
with the gunshot in his temple, the third eye,
the last circle."

You are running down Summit Avenue in the dark:
harmony and the moon and the screaming girl.

The woman in your dream says,
"It was an accident in my life.
Give me a candy bar.

Give me your baby for my loving toy.
Honey, give me that baby and let's see
the Christmas tree now. I like the light
on the silver threads."

I can live with the kindest man who ever loved me.
I can run the streets of my city in the perfect air
that surrounds my life.
Trains still frighten me, and the dark circle we lived in,
that too, and I can speak with this voice as I run,
but I hear the young woman speaking from the single bed,
from the small room she almost got lost in
so many years ago, she says,

"You break my heart
in the moonlight.
You fill me with such desire.
I am afraid of you. Hold me."

Stigmata

Seven times in my life I had lesions in the center
of my left palm. Before I read about saints
I hated those opened places, lines of blood,
and faithfully applied cream and bandages
each night before sleep. I made no connection
with these marks and Christ's death because
I was a girl, was not taught such drama
was available to me.

When I grew up I studied to become a Catholic
and discovered girl and women saints.
I thought about those lattice marks I'd carried
in my palms, wishing them back, but they have
never returned.

I would like someone I love to cut long strips
of white linen and wrap my hands very tenderly
a few moments each month.
I would not like my hands to be bleeding or in disarray,
I would just like that gentle treatment.

The Autobiography of Clothes

I cannot find the red hat everyone tells me I must buy.
You know the one, the hat that frames my face, makes me
medieval and righteous and wanton at once, the red hat
like a poppy gone wild in a blaze of summer.

And my wedding blouse. Hungry for a body inside. White satin
glowing in the prosaic closet. Believe my skin deserves
to wear it more than once. Believe in my skin against
white satin, in white.

There's the old New Balance shoes I can't give up. Nothing
left of their clever construction, paper thin, sorry sights.
I am standing in my oldest son's room, August 13, 1984, 6 P.M.,
wearing the old shoes, and go into labor.

The water breaks, shoes saturated, these shoes, the ones
I don't throw at the cats, these shoes I've walked in for miles
never thinking of my father, these shoes I've worn searching
for the perfect red hat.

But I cannot find it. The wedding blouse gives up on me,
waits for a new bride full of promise and light,
and you said to me, coming into the basement late one night,
"What are you doing?" but I could hardly hear you,

wrapped in fabrics I've collected for twenty years,
I couldn't hear you say, "You look beautiful, that dark red
wool against the brown corduroy against your white skin."
Is that what you said? I couldn't hear anything you said

to me, so protected by the layers of unsewn fabric,
all that cloth without shape or judgement circling around me.

Marriage

Long ago I came through the prairie,
mountains broke from the earth and rose
up. I was afraid and said the prairie was
finished.

I do not follow the blood blue line
on the map that would lead me to the San Juan mountains.
I assume they do not exist, have little to teach me.
I drive in a circle, a complicated and beautiful circle,
and prairie, prairie, prairie is my choice, is all I see.

Feverish

Golden leaves the only currency—
their value rises as wind carries them
away from our greedy pockets.

Autumn and everyone says: Don't you love autumn?
Autumn is my favorite season. Don't you wish autumn
would last a little longer?

I used to press them in the dictionary. Find them
in spring by *Catalpa* and *repentance*.
Find them by *mourning* and *obscure*.
Maybe not money but the gold of an apprentice painter,
the one who never figured out how to get back to Venice,
who trailed paintings behind her, left them as payment
for safe rooms to sleep in during summer heat.

When Dutch Elm disease destroyed the streets of our city
we were given one chance to prove ourselves worthy
of new trees: East and West, Sugar Maples—in autumn
they make twilight ferocious. North and South—Red Maples.
They bore me, but they have lived.
If all the new trees live they will help me forget
why I can't leave the city.

The trees are changing. Last night I fell asleep
and my favorite tree was golden. I woke at 3 A.M.,
turned on the alley light, my tree
had turned red in the night, inside of the heart,
open and jagged, but feeling something.

All the cats look feverish and afraid of deprivation.
I used to love the way the truth of their jungle
history guided them with wit, their vagrant purposefulness,
urgent, closer to the earth than mine.

"I'm sad," he said, "Don't get me wrong, I'm not depressed.
I'm just calling to say the world is a sad, sad place."

The golden leaves circle my yard. I'm embattled.
My forehead is hot but there's no fever.

Amnesia Plague

You thought it was only you. You couldn't remember the day
your father died. Felt subhuman. But, your best friend

forgot her own anniversary, her husband didn't leave but wanted
to, and your oldest daughter walked down the stairs into

a mother's day celebration, left quickly, returning later
with a card made from whatever materials were available

in her cloistered room—a row of flowers, pink and orange,
only, construction paper faded by edgy winter sun. She said

she was planning to skip father's day too, no offense. Lately
you can barely remember Greece, how the wind came into

the harbor, how your body swore never to leave. The airplane
that carried you away was pure fiction. Someone else said

she couldn't remember how many lovers she'd had, but her health
was holding up so she didn't worry about amnesia, though

others now make the lover list in terror, the phone calls
made with honor though the mortal news is the newest version

of the telegram edged in black. Someone kind said it was late
October, don't you remember you're always in despair right

before November? No, I don't remember that. No one can
remember where they put their winter hats or gloves, we can't

find the Frosty the Snowman mittens that make winter acceptable,
we can't remember who wrote Canada's national anthem, can't

remember all the words though the melody stays clear. On
Bishop's desert island Crusoe holds a fragment of poetry in his

fragile mind, he may look it up years later, and Mungoshi's line, "If
you don't stay bitter and angry for too long . . ." what? If I

don't, then . . . and I don't, not for too long. It was never about
bitterness, or crossing the boundary of the page, it wasn't

about my father or my family, or the memorable dates that slip
from the angelic calendar, bereft of the idea of sanctuary,

what they meant now meaningless. The plague was different,
mortal terror of a muted sort, a privileged horror,

terrible vacancies though no one seemed to be dying.

after Charles Baxter,
after Garcia–Márquez

How I Walk

I walk with my keys inserted
    between each space
in my hand. I use only two
    keys in my real life
but keep two from some past lives
    I've led so I can have
all four spaces filled.

    I lace my keys between the fingers
        of my left hand, my power
    hand, the hand strong from writing,
        the hand strong because it's
    connected to my strongest arm, strong
        left arm that's carried my babies.

So now I'm walking. Can you see me?
    I am a big woman, and I walk fast.
If you look closely you can see the glint
    of the tips of my keys. It's a flash,
not like a diamond. I don't have diamonds;
    it's four flashes: light   light
light   light. When I come home from walking
    my fist is cramped from keeping
the tips of my keys at attention.

    I'm older now, have too many jobs,
        I don't walk four miles a day any more.
    When I walk now all I see are dogs
        connected to women by metal chains,
    leather chains, so really I think of them
        as dog-chained-women, or maybe women-
    chained-dogs. I no longer reach out
        my hand, palm up, to any dog,

the women have told me they do not want
    their dogs to make friends
with strangers. These women tied to dogs
    are all sizes. Some are tall as I am,
some taller, some have warrior faces,
    some cupid faces, some have lines
putting new faces on top of old faces,
    some are shockingly beautiful,
some are tiny.

Tiny women connected to dogs
    always made sense to me.
These tiny women are vulnerable,
    I thought, so many years
ago. I thought, tiny women must be
    frightened. I have always
had, in my circle of women, tiny
    women friends. Tiny meaning:
perfect, to me, a big woman. One
    small friend of mine just
wrote a brilliant essay about walking
    in a woman's body; one dearest
small friend, raped years ago,
    no dog in the apartment
to take the knife in her place.

Whenever I walk with that friend
    I've always thought,
she is safe with me. I am big and walk
    with extraordinary purpose.
If someone came toward us with menace
    as we walked the circle of
the lake, I know I would kill that person,
    would hurl my key hand into
his eye, his delicate throat, and I would
    tell my friend to run to the

nearest tree and climb it and I would find
    her in the branches, my keys would
be bloody, my hand damaged but still full
    of power.

I walk with my keys and pretend
    they give me all I need.
I pretend because I have size I will
    always be safe. Some friends
of mine who are small have never
    been attacked. Some friends
of mine, my size, have been raped and beaten.
    If I think about this I might
stop walking. And I was not there
    to save my friend the night
she was cut and raped. I have not been able
    to save friends, children, strangers.

How I walk is with my keys, alone
    or with a friend, I walk
full of vengeance and denial, I walk
    in fear where once I walked
in poetry, in love, in the light
    of the blessed sun, the blessed moon.

Thanksgiving Night/1991

—For Joe, Cass, and Bren

It's late but there's four chapters left
of *The Lion, The Witch & The Wardrobe.*
I've been reading the story for weeks now,
and tonight Aslan is being tortured and killed.

Joe's room is wrapped in Christmas lights all year.
It's one way we dismiss darkness; the lights
are his beauty and his need. Aslan is dying now
and Joe is still under the covers.

Brendan's home from college for Thanksgiving.
We're all a little stunned to see him again,
to feel him alive in the house. He drops down
on the extra bed to listen to the story.

The golden lion dies on a stone table. My sons,
so many years apart, with their own gold hair
listen to my voice carry the narrative. Cass,
my nephew, has come up from Chicago for Thanks-

giving, walks in now, two chapters later, lured
from TV laughs downstairs by what? My low voice,
the possibility of resurrection? Tiredness after
a long day of family and too much bounty? He rests

beside Brendan as the story gathers toward its
inevitable, disguised Christian joy. A boy,
two young men, a reader—a novel ends, a lion rises
up, the comfort in the room is excruciating,

its lyric quality makes my heart almost sick
with gratitude. I have been afraid of forgetting
this moment I was allowed to have. Joe slept then,
and already I cannot remember where we other three went.

The New Planet

In late November Brendan and Mary draped the front of the house
with Christmas lights: flashing whites on running tracks,

traditional orange and gold, red and blue bulbs the size of
real people's noses. It's February and last night I sat

in my hot car outside my own house. I was so tired from teaching
and the baby inside me was cramped and wanted out and who

could blame it? When Dylan started singing I just started
crying. The new planet is so cold, and I don't feel like myself

living here. His voice was the bulletin from where I used to
live; I was stunned he could make it through the black waves

of air, the meteor showers all the way to me. On the new planet
I don't play Salt Lake Solitaire anymore. I can't even

remember how I used to spend my time, my hands don't bleed
from the shuffle, nobody even wants to play Hearts

with me, and if I don't teach my children soon, no one
here will know any of the old games that made me happy.

One of the women in the song was leaning toward the Jack
of Hearts when I turned off the car. The Christmas lights

reflected in all the windows, I was wrapped in color and
racing white light. I was glad they had let me bring

my family to the new planet. Now that the song was over
I remembered that at least our house was safe for now.

Cordelia: One Portrait at a Time

In a faded velvet chair holding Cordelia.
She is drowsy, giving up her madcap stomp,
barely awake, small river of milk
pulled into her belly by her rose mouth.

In a faded velvet chair holding Cordelia
the bottle goes from white to transparent,
the air bubbles remind me of the ocean,
the lonely tourists going down, the trace
of breath they give away in their dying.

In a faded velvet chair holding Cordelia.
Her eyelashes drop, the fringe of black,
small gates brushing shut, and her body
sinks deeper into my body, we wait,

and in a faded velvet chair holding Cordelia
I finally shift and rise, her blanket
sweeps behind us, robe, wedding veil,
wave and murmur, asleep and alive she breathes.

White Mittens

—*for Christina Baldwin*

The woman wore white
mittens as she flung
the laundry across
the clothesline, white
sheets sailed and slumped
on the cold rope,
her daughter's pajamas
hung limp, her husband's
white T-shirts swung,
benign masculine flags,
her mittens signaled
up and down as her body
bent to the clothes
basket, then lifted
what was still waiting
to be hung and when
the hunter's bullet
entered her body
she didn't have the
chance to say, "Don't
shoot, I'm a woman,
not a deer, I have
so much work left
to do."
And in the forest
we drove down a
narrow road and on
one side a doe,
on the other a doe,

and in the back flank
of one a perfect white
arrow, the tip imbedded
like a deep human kiss,
a message she was carrying
and the arrow hadn't killed
her, aimed so closely at
the turned-up white tail,
the only deer sign of
vulnerability, the arrow
swayed like an awful message
she was made to carry
into the winter forest,
and she would not let us
close enough to pull it from
her body, though we knew
we were innocent and
available.

The Snow Woman

Melted suddenly and was gone.
I saw her carrot nose. I saw her red yarn
mouth before the gray bird picked it up
and flew away. Her mouth makes his nest now.

The snow woman was a beauty. Everyone said so.
We did her in a ballgown so we wouldn't have to
carve her legs.

We put my old black dancing shoes
on the ground in front of her. As the sun
took her the shoes filled with water.

The snow woman had cranberries for hair,
ripped from the cranberry tree. She was not
flirtatious, but solemn; however, the red color
was great against the white.

Before she melted there was an amazing snowstorm.
She was buried and formless—shaggy—for three days
she wasn't really a woman until the wind blew the storm
off her body. Her yarn mouth hung down after the wind.
We went out and fixed her. She looked like a caught fish
for that moment.

When she melted the backyard felt empty and boring,
like when your beloved brothers leave for college,
and there's no one to talk to late at night.

None of us talked to her. We just lived with her.
We built her with arms lifted, ready to embrace us.

COLOPHON

The text of this book was set in Spectrum and Albertus MT type-faces. It was printed on acid-free paper, and smyth sewn for durability and reading comfort.